Downshifting

by Adrian Buckner

Downshifting

by Adrian Buckner

Five Leaves Publications
www.fiveleaves.co.uk

Downshifting
by Adrian Buckner

Published in 2017 by Five Leaves,
14a Long Row, Nottingham NG1 2DH

www.fiveleaves.co.uk
www.fiveleavesbookshop.co.uk

ISBN 978-1910170328

Typeset and designed by
Four Sheets Design and Print

Printed in Great Britain

Contents

I

II

III

IV

V

I

Downshifting

Today I took the stairs, bearing only
the lingering touch of shutdown
on my index finger, the half dozen
novels I salvaged from the shelves
and Peter's last words to me:
he needs to run something past me,
get my take, can we do coffee?
Yes, tomorrow, tomorrow is ok.
Yes, that's right, a little bed time reading
and yes, no rest for you, wicked man.

I walked into the park: back against trunk
gazing into the canopy; but in truth,
the free sylvan spirit is really not my thing.
There's my place beneath the stars:
a man smoking outside an Industrial Unit.
He said come back tomorrow night,
punch this card into that wall,
take a broom and sweep this pile over to there.
When you've finished, sit and wait for me
and remember to bring something to read.

Mary Ann, delineate for me every stitch
of her dress, every clarity and confusion
in the heart and mind of your Dorothea.
For her I will push piles of debris from
one corner of the warehouse to its opposite.
Charlotte, stay with me, send me home
with your desperate Jane, my head
with hers on the soft moss, inclining
to the beading rain on the bus window.
Thomas, I am with you in the dead hour,
perched on my forklift truck, watching
Egdon Heath turn to dusk in six pages.
Marcel, don't fall asleep. It is only page thirty five,
mama is at the foot of the stairs
and tea breaks are long on the nightshift.
Holden Caulfield, give me every word
of that David Copperfield kind of crap.
You can have for your next breakdown
my chair on the ninth floor.
I vacated it today. I took the stairs.

Empty University

What shall I do?
Maybe pull up that poem
and decide once and for all
between a stop and semicolon
in line five.
I think there might
be more wrong with it
than I have the capacity
to see right now.
After all,
I wrote it thirteen years ago.
What did I know thirteen years ago?
What do I know now
about what I knew thirteen years ago?
I'll wander over to the window
and look at the tennis court
where my son
who is sixteen
beat me for the first time.
Someone down the corridor
is telling one of the admin. workers
how wonderful Greece was
and how he is finding it more difficult
every year to crank up for the new term.
Not having had a day off for three months,
she declines to comment.
What shall I do?
I think I will type out *Bonjour Tristesse*
and teach it to the first years —
every comma and ache of it.

'Provide brief bullet points of your specific Research Specialisms'

Running back to school after lunch
I fell and gashed my knee.

A neighbour took me home,
delivering a beautiful afternoon.

I watched a cinema I'd never entered
being demolished in the High Street.

When I heard Gabrielle Fitzpatrick
had *split her head open* I blanched

at the vision, avoided for good
that legendary spot.

I fell in love with cricket. It rained
three summers and hardly happened.

I was worse than thirty-third
in a subject called Technical Drawing.

I went from altar boy to feminist,
having no sex twice.

At University I went to no lectures,
read all the Russians and Hardy.

I thought about teaching,
then thought again.

I slept in the afternoon, woke
to the lilies past their seven days.

'List examples of the actual or likely "impact" of your research on the wider community (non-academic)'

The wider community is my only community.
My wider community is not a wide one.

Charles, sufficiently forbearing
to read my poems for the last fifteen years
will likely point to my erratic use of the comma –
then tactfully broaden the discussion
to embrace tone and cadence.
The actual impact on Charles is not easy to quantify.
He may think about my poem a few days later,
or remember something else he wanted to say
about how it might be improved.
He will take time to tell me.
This is the heart of our friendship.
I think it is likely to endure
whatever impacts are snooping around.

Alex has cheerfully resigned himself
to the fact that I will never write
the poems he thinks I should be writing.
He has given up arguing with me.
In hospital after a heart attack,
he wrote a hundred prose poems
that I did not understand.
His views on poetry have no impact
on how I write my poems;
my views have no impact on how he writes his.
We have been exchanging poems for two decades.
I think it very likely
we will continue for at least another two.

You found something

You found something in the room
where poetry was taught –
an image boiling

with precision,
a perfect break
in a line.

You came back after five minutes,
in a fluster from the lift.
Is the room still open?

I hope you found your pen,
your umbrella, your purse…
and will ask you, if I remember.

Someone asked Chekhov
where he got his ideas.
He said, 'Pass me that ashtray' –

felt the weight of it and then …
'Tomorrow I will have a story
for you, 'The ashtray'.

The Story

I could see the smallest things
by Raymond Carver

Another year, another September
and another red rollerball pen.
Another note in the margin
to mark another reason why
he said, I said, he said, I said
is the way things are said.
Another daub of yellow highlighter
through the space between the lines,
another word found bearing
the weight of human sorrow.

Handing copies round for the fifth year
in a row, I thought of you,
hundreds of miles from here now,
embracing the huge promise of your life.
'What happens in this story?' I'd asked.
You spoke first: urgent, shy,
hand only half raised, but eyes
to the far horizon where you always
could see the smallest things:
'A woman realises she is unhappy.'

The Summative Assessment

(for a student of poetry)

From the two lines you have shown me
I see you bear the sweet curse of poetry.

Your work will never be done.
Time runs out behind College walls,

run outs and runs out again beyond them.
Embrace your forever *formative* world:

whisper what you have written
a hundred times on waking,

a hundred times at the bus stop
and in the park you cut through.

Come to class but stay mute. Listen for
the nightingale. Do not ignore the owl.

"I'd forgotten how much I love this poem"

Hello, said the poem, how have you been?
I've been waiting for you, I haven't changed.
Did my author die? For real or just in
the seminar? Never mind all that now.

You've been out there amid blurred things –
the flashy plots of contemporary novels,
papers from students eager to advance
your argument with the honoured dead.

Then a real death, a house to clear,
a life to face. Take your time –
let my climate enfold you, my landscape
clarify and come into view again

on the heavy grained imprint,
blot-filling a void in *e*, a void in *d.*

Consolation

For Huw Watkins

Dear Huw, thank you
for sending *Love Poem*.
I am, as they say,
delighted to accept
Love Poem for publication
in the small circulation
poetry magazine
which, as they also say,
I am privileged to edit.
(By the way, 'accepting'
in the sense
of accepting poetry
will be, from today,
my favourite use
of that word –
imagine a world,
or even one street,
where everyone spent
a minute each day
accepting a poem).
    If I was better
at avoiding cliché
when telling poets
what I like about their poems
I would avoid saying
that *Love Poem*
possesses a rare delicacy;
but alas, I am not

so allow me to say
that *Love Poem*
possesses so rare a delicacy
that I thought
for one moment
as I gazed at it
the words might slip away
from the page
where you have set them
so elegantly,
and lose themselves
on a stray breeze
into the garden
which that afternoon,
for no other reason
than my looking
out at it
was the green, stilling
heart of melancholy.

Leaving *Love Poem*
on the kitchen table,
I went out to collect
my son from the school gate,
noticing on my way
the noisy progress
of grass being dug up
by yellow machinery
in a warming instance
of neighbourly collaboration.
What a weight off
to be able at last
to pull the car

up off the street,
to not have to
mow the lawn,
or look out at it.

Well, I suppose
if I don't like it
I can, as they say,
lump it,
get out of earshot
and intone-whisper
to myself
those lines
from *Love Poem*
that I have already
by heart.

The following afternoon,
reading *Love Poem* again,
I noticed something
that in my oblivion of whimsy
I had missed:

Yet when a petal falls//
from this dying rose
it is of no consolation
to think of mountains

I pondered
how though we might say
'of no account',
'of no consequence',
this *of* is surplus
in its connection
to *no consolation*.

Looking out still
at my green, suburban
heart of melancholy,
I came reluctantly
to the conclusion
that I would communicate
to you this editorial quibble.

In, as they would say,
this day and age, when
as I would say,
you can barely hear yourself
accepting a poem,
let alone whisper-intoning
it to yourself,
it is perhaps
of no account,
of no consequence
that two men might
debate a preposition
in a poem called *Love Poem*
that one of them has written
and which will be lost
between the covers
of a small circulation
poetry magazine
edited by the other.
Of no consequence,
of no account,
but perhaps
some consolation.

Lest We Channel Hop

The Great War   BBC 1964
(repeat broadcast, spring 2005)

The Great War dragged on,
slugging through the schedule
between Lunchtime News and Tots TV.

Stalled, it dug in for weeks,
stalemated at World Snooker fortnight,
Championship Golf and Campaign Specials,

before heaving itself
into May's final push.
Would it ever end?

Life on the Home Front was as normal,
though sometimes they could be heard
above the boom of suburban mowers,

those daytime TV voices:
Redgrave narrating, Williams
as Lloyd George and Richardson, Haig.

II

Anna Karenina's Mobile

I must speak to you, come at once
But your telegram, Anna, flies where?
I was to blame. Come home.
But your note, Anna, misses the hour.

The child hammers the table, stares
blankly from black-currant eyes
then rings out its laughter
to remind you of him.

You must go somewhere,
updating every minute
between hope and despair
with your maddened tweets –

the bold, ugly young men,
the beggar woman with a baby,
the boys and their dirty ice cream –

all flung into the world
only to hate each other

and driving you now
to another platform end,
recalling that first one, since when
it's been pay, pay, pay as you go.

The words of Leo Tolstoy (*Anna Karenina, trans: Louise & Aylmer Maude*) are woven into the text of this poem

Tolstoy on Bus Route 38

I couldn't put it down!

For three chapters Constantine Levin
casts love and trouble aside,
picks up a scythe
and taking the offered kvas
helps the peasants mow his fields
in the hottest part of the day.

How readable, how put-downable,
how exquisitely discrete,
the two hundred and thirty-nine
chapters of *Anna Karenina.*

I too can cast love and trouble aside,
just as today, I can turn my gaze
from the caress stab on smart phones,
the discarded litter of free news.

Levin returns happy from the field.
I put him down, look out the window
at the passing succession of plaques
on Derby's Edwardian Villas:

Thirlmere Dorothy
St. James Eden Park

One for the notebook, Count Leo –
what of Dorothy Thirlmere
taking her morning walk
in St James and Eden Park?

And look with me now
– the free, alighted passenger –
into this park
at mid-morning:

a three-year-old pockets
the conker he has found.
The rest of the world
has gone over the hill.

A world scattered
with discrete chapters;

world put-downable,
windows to look out –

this would be life
were it mine to distil.

Bed Time Reading

Anna Karenina

For Kay

Twenty-six years since you inscribed
ownership, dated the title page

and made a thousand marks
on Tolstoy's eight hundred.

I fan through, breathe
the neat scholarly intent

of your voracious pencil, its expectant
trawl for character.

You told me you read the whole thing
in three days. This still amazes me

and I want you to tell me again.
But ten minutes ago you dropped

The War Against Cliché by your side of the bed,
kissed me and fell asleep instantly.

So I turn on my side, wondering about
the books that couples keep of themselves,

the bold of early markings, the fading
pages, the confiding quiet of years.

Bed Time Reading

Fathers and Sons

Ivan Sergeyevich, I think I may love you
for reasons that are not the best:

Pavel Petrovich is right – the early days of June
are the most beautiful of the year;

they are also the loveliest in which
to re-read your masterpiece.

I burnt slowly in the back garden,
turning the last seventy pages,

eyeing the lilac abuzz and blue,
finding Bazarov impossible to love.

Only now, by lamplight, can I enter
those grievous arguments of yours

with the young nihilist: your duelling,
loving, dying Yevgeny.

Bed Time Reading

The Brothers Karamazov

Mitya, I want only to judge you
at your own pleading estimate:
a blackguard but no thief; lover
of sweet gutter life, no parricide.

Downstairs, piled on the piano stool –
a dozen promises on paper.
Here with you, criminal of honest heart:
rainbow rolls of roubles, hopeless need for her.

Poem at Christmas ending with a line from George Eliot

On Christmas Eve I woke thinking
about the copy of *Middlemarch*

– Penguin English Library, 1978 –
I left on my desk at the University.

On Christmas Day I woke thinking
about it again, or rather just seeing

it there, front cover detached, waiting
to be sellotaped when I read it again

at Easter or in the summer. I like
to see it there, orange heft of spine

resuming calm, rightful possession
of that quiet place.

On Boxing Day I woke thinking
about the Adult Education classes,

the church crypt in a Midlands town,
where we gathered every week

with individual volumes
of the Penguin English Library

to make notes in the margin amid
the roar on the other side of silence.

*If we had a keen vision and feeling for ordinary human life, it would be
like hearing the grass grow and the squirrel's heart beat, and we should
die of that roar which lies on the other side of silence.*

Middlemarch

The Great Stories

"Oh, you're reading her too! Isn't she wonderful?
Yes, you've got the *Selected*, I've got the new one.
Twelve collections now, is it? Yes,
what an achievement, such an eye for detail.

I just love the one where the man leaves
the Northern town and you never find out...
yes, and the one, what *is* it called? –
where the woman loses her three children
and mourns only one, the middle one? –
or no, maybe..."

    I'll never forget her, the 514 biro'd
    into her wrist, the hole in her jeans,
    the auburn curls, freckles, and the quiet
    we shared for the last ten minutes on the train

while I looked away and at nothing –
how they all go I thought,
so deeply into us, but too far
past that useful shallower place.

Love Tweets to Naturalism

"Zola's naturalism is ugly and dirty,
but he seems to me to be *doing something*"
Henry James

Theodore,
may I hibernate with you?
Émile,
make my duvet of your pages?

I am back in love with you –
the huge heave
of your grossly humane project,
your vast attention span.

I will read you
in the small hours,
browse your footnotes
till dawn.

Here
I fell asleep
Will I dream
a comprehended world?

To be returned to

On June fourteenth, nineteen sixty six, Matlock's College of Education Library took into their care and shelved Robert Lowell's *For the Union Dead.*

Sometime after June sixth, nineteen eighty four Matlock's College Library DISCARDED the same.

On August fourth, two thousand and fifteen, a literary academic, retiring at Christmas and unable to house his library, identified me as a home for Lowell – gifting me what had been gifted him sometime after June sixth, nineteen eighty four.

Hardback first edition, second impression; between shelving date and discarding date there are seven *To be returned by* stamps, though – 5 MAY 1975 comes twice, the second a heavy right way up correction, so bold it scared off lenders for nine years.

A new anthology above my head proclaims a new golden age for poetry – so many new voices reaching so many new readers who can write their own new poems by working through fifty new exercises to be found a little further along the shelf.

I admired my Teachers, fresh out of University, burning with zeal for a clutch of key single authored collections, Lowell's *Union Dead* perhaps the most essential, lost then to my weak understanding.

But with its added poem – a thin tombstone of seven date stamp lines, composed over eighteen years and left three decades in an academic's cave – no longer lost to me, though discarded and dispersed amid the new.

Why I tend to avoid it

Okay, I thought, I really should try it;
though I am quite a happy dinosaur
propped up in bed

reading, thinking, dozing.

So I typed in *For the Union Dead*
– that grieving civility – looking, I think
for that dishonoured brand of Crit. –

Appreciation. Four scrolls down,
someone is calling someone else a cunt.

III

The Football Obituary

Thirty thousand men in caps
willed him spring-heeled
above the ruined February pitch

to make that header – yes,
that header
in the quarter final against City.

A single International –
an injustice
still embraced over pints in town.

A One Club man:
the brief stint in charge,
the scouting, the youth team,

the failed haulage business;
that unfortunate misunderstanding
at the North End Gate.

A statement was issued.
He was always welcome.
The minute silence.

That header. *That* header.

Northern Love, 1970

(BBC2 Rugby League Floodlit Trophy)

Not *Lundy, Fastnet, Irish Sea;*
not *Montrose, Brechin*
and *Stenhousemuir;*

not Malin, Hebrides,
Fair Isle, Faeroes;
not *Cowdenbeath 3* or *St. Mirren 2.*

Though they chimed mainly fair
and stilled the lullable child,
there were stranger, less distant places

in my heart, planted
by a year of second halves
in the land of three channels only:

Dewsbury, Swinton, Keighley;
Widnes, Warrington, Wigan;
Salford, Batley and *Leigh.*

Barrow, Castleford, St. Helens;
Bramley, Hunslet and *Huyton.*
Not a word have I inscribed

with more placing care,
such pencil-erasered love,
as the winner

of my imaginary league:
Featherstone. Featherstone Rovers.
How I longed to rove

across the feather stone,
over stone feathers,
the feathers of stone.

Do not tell me
of the catastrophe of coal,
that feather means four in Old English

and the church bell
is only feet off the ground;
for little have I roved

in my forty nine years
from *Whitehaven* and *Wakefield,*
from *Rochdale* where *Hornets* fly,

from the *KR* in *Hull*
so little have I roved
so little have I roved.

The Making of Me

England versus Australia, Kennington Oval, August 1975

1.

Nothing so green as that patch
beneath the smoke of SE 11;

so neglected as Vauxhall Station,
encrusted and flaking with disuse;

so sedate as the hours of play,
the outfield pigeons unstirred;

so empty as the fifteen thousand seats
dotted with four hundred spectators;

less fathomable than my desire to stay, gazing
for the first time into the core of something –

stilled by the resolving dissonance, never
to be rooted out of me

by fastidious village greens, their congruent
pavilions and obliging spires.

2.

A month past my thirteenth birthday I sat
five days out of six on a slatted wooden bench

watching the longest cricket match
ever played in England.

The sun shone all week, I burnt
slowly and barely spoke at all.

Across the parched green, two huge gasholders
though I seldom looked up there.

I dawdled back to Vauxhall,
the dirt of London clung,

behind me, forever in me,
the longest cricket match

ever played in England
had finished in a draw.

3.

In the single carriage, I sank
into the comfortably broken seat,

ranged my pencils and rulers
to check the figures and scores.

Outside, what I knew
but didn't understand – London,

stuck in post war, belching
as much filth as it still could.

The high rises and tarmac courts
flash vanished to the gardens

of Putney and Richmond. At home
I wrote down someone else's words:

The Australians cursed the sluggish turf.
A draw played out on a featherbed.

From *Love Me Do* to Altamont

For Simon Philo *

Born in '62, but not
into a house of music,

I found, not The Beatles
in the air, but for myself

in '72: *Crazy Horses* –
my first 45 for 45 pence.

A year later (aeons! aeons!)
my purchase of *Life On Mars*

nudged it up one place to four
on Tuesday's lunchtime chart.

What beautiful wastes
of languid childish time

measured by one side of Santana,
my consciously chosen band.

Now in middle age
it stings afresh to know

from your labour
of scholarship and love:

that deeper seam
behind and beyond,

from *Love Me Do* to Altamont
passed in a crushing blink.

British Invasion: The Crosscurrents of Musical Influence.
Rowman & Littlefield, 2015

Love at First Words

In Memory of Richie Benaud and John Arlott –
the game, the words, the spirit

when I heard
Snow made hay under grey skies

when Illingworth opted
for an exploratory over of spin

when play paused
for movement behind the bowler's arm

when Luckhurst and Edrich
accepted the offered light

So I sought the legends and lore
on the second-hand shelves –

gazed on the comradely grace
of Benaud and Worrell
when battle was done;

Hutton's victory wave in '53 –
the slow wide smile, the easy formality,
the cigarette in his right hand.

(Four Byes)

1. A Losing Draw

Did you win?
No, we held on
for a losing draw.

What's a losing draw?
It's when the game isn't finished
but if it had been
we'd have lost.

So, the other team…?
They get a winning draw.
If they'd been a bit better
they'd have won.

So who is happier?
Hard to say.
It depends on
how you feel about
all that other stuff –
marriage, relationships with kids,
work, back pain, not being able
to drink much anymore…

*And how do you feel about
all that other stuff?*
I don't think about it
when I'm playing cricket.

Perhaps you should?
Prefer not to,
reminds me too much
of losing draws.

2. The Well-Bred Nought

Greets the keeper and surveys the scene,
taps the crease with a touch of suspicion,
blocks a straight one with text book precision.
Adjusts his guard, takes note of the spire,
then nicks a lifter for a catch sharp but clean.

3. On the occasion of his wicket keeping début for Derbyshire (over 50s)
versus Cheshire 20.5.2015

A joy absurd, but the no less profound –
being not so much selected – as found.

4. London, 2012 ...

... Wimbledon screaming,
Ashes fever.

Don't worry, all of that passes.

Rain still falls
on the pocked tarmac court.

Someone somewhere can't find
a six for the scoreboard,
makes do with a wrong way nine.

A six year old in Barcelona kit
kicks penalties in the rain past his Dad.

IV

Running, after three years

I am your stitch. I come one mile in.
Drag me home another half mile.

Drag me through the last three years,
through that venomous promotion,

the corridors of dull enmity,
their midnight blinking screens.

Drag me through the cluttered outhouse
and the shut door dumping room,

past brave words misremembered
and a promise now reframed.

Drag me through new sympathies
of back pain and sleeplessness.

Drag me toward that distant train
across the breaking dawn,

I'll drive from you a stride for home
where you'll sink

to the grasp above your knees
and heave the whole of it.

Go for a 15-minute walk.
Think about your life
and what you want from it.

The Independent "The No-Diet Diet"

The hedge in the lane needs cutting back.
I remember thinking the same last year

when I last decided I needed to shake
myself out of this. Looking forward,

I'd like to arrange my succession
of defeats into decorous verse

on a white page – couplets preferably,
those lovely horizontal margins.

And when they've been second-hand shelved,
I'd like a young man to take them up,

turn to his lover and say
Look, this is beautiful.

And she'd say, *Yes, but we*
won't ever be like that, will we?

The sunburnt poem

is dedicated to a girl,
now over fifty and living overseas;

was written in ten minutes
and dated at the foot of the page;

lay half the afternoon
next to someone else's *Collected Poems*

one Tuesday in August
when the poet's wife was at work;

will never be typed
but might be sent somewhere;

has two words deleted,
a comma shifted

and ends with the poet
asleep in the shade.

The Esplanade Chair

One of the world's smaller tokens –
a punched out numbered ticket,

valid that whole afternoon
and left in a novel.

Not much reading was done,
gazing across the wide blue of the bay

at the shining years,
the small creeping despairs.

Shining years,
slow creeping despairs.

Both must fray –
shining years, fragile despairs,

gazing across
the wide blue of a bay.

The Trees

In truth, I know very little about trees.
Only in the spring of your coming home
was I stirred to look, read and learn.

So my guesses were mostly wrong
when we took that walk in the afternoon.
Today, I walked there again –

lime flowers on Markeaton Road,
marble apples on Wheeldon Avenue –
my strewn, sentimental homework.

I want to show it all to you,
reel off the correct names
and gain your big approving tick.

July

    July, July

I wrote you poems in a wet July,
on each morning's leaf
a beading drop of rain.
A year on
England is scorched and pale
and this afterthought of love
drains a summer's cup of verse.

    July, July, July

Pale, unstirred –
cut grass has lain three weeks.
Might all the Julys
left to me
stay dry?
I would look back, beyond
to the soft rain,
the softer, softer rain,
the longer, longer month,
the younger, younger you.

An Airing for Love

A song of love breathes
from a window
on the city's lassitude.

I make out each word,
learnt when grief was borrowed
and love overstated.

Now the keening voice
drifts from profundity;
a simple strain of regret,

a wafted note
seeping from a raised sash
to blend with the cat,

the clamorous street game,
and the cares of parents
urging restraint.

Fascination   Everything But The Girl, 1984

This Afternoon

after C.J. Allen's "This Morning"
and Philip Larkin's "Home"

I am glad I did not go to work.
I went to work instead
on cleaning the rabbit hutch
and re-stocking the bird feeder.

I do not know the names of clouds
but watched them anyway
and thought about how you put *feelings*
and *sad* in one short poem,

how this is not like you,
though it may be a little like you
since *beech leaves* and *suburban gardens*
are there too. Those beech leaves.

One More Thing

She looks out to the tulips,
he re-reads a headline.

Things lie too deep
to be *talked through*

but would be nothing
for the touch

he cannot give
to the moment.

A gift lost
or never his?

He only knows
it is one more thing

he wants her
to do for him.

Pinned

by every terse star
in the clear February night,
a man –
hands plunged, eyes down,
hastening from the hospital gate.

In Saint Peter's, Nottingham

I sit in the south aisle of Saint Peter's,
figuring out the stained glass:

Christ's entry into Jerusalem, the upbraiding
of the chastened money-men.

As a child that anger was portrayed
to me as sweepingly, lashingly physical

but here is stilled into the coldness
of shadeless colour and glass.

A heavy man in heavy rags approaches me:
Are you praying? No, I'm here for a little quiet

I say with a smile but sour intent.
Hungry? No, I've just eaten thank you.

Go on, have a sweet with me – he offers
an unopened tube of mints.

Thank you, I say. He touches
my shoulder, shuffles off

to no sort of welcome elsewhere.
I dawdle back through the crowds.

Go on he echoes in my head
have a sweet with me.

Evan Dando

For Tom

You peer out to us
but long hair veils
what we might see in your eyes.

Lumberjack shirt
across that broad chest
seems like plain statement.

Rooted rock still
far left of the stage,
not hewn granite

but playing the sediments
of pain, sinking still
to find their levels.

Derby, 21st April 2012

Love poems

Some are only written
because the lover
wants to write words
he would not usually use
like *My Love* and *Forever*.
They fit into envelopes,
have a handwritten address
and postage stamps
are required
to convey them.
They are not
the apparently artless,
they are artless.
They don't deserve
the name of poetry
and there is really
no reason to write them
other than that they come
before love turns into
a starved, bloated thing.
They come early
when love
is making its own love
with joy.
Mostly, they are worthless.
Like all writing
they end with a
word and a stop
and this is one
of those poems of love.

Darling, meet me by some water

My inclination is
to write you a love poem
in the time honoured

contemporary style.
There might be a moon in it,
or a sun westering

below an urban roof,
but mostly it would fix
on interior details –

the rented
space we share,
all the grimy lyrical things

that lie around
when we wake
in the evening after red wine and love.

But poets
have re-discovered rivers
and their flowing,

deeper selves.
Confluence
is now an important word

and I feel a little shallow
in our entire, sealed
content.

So Darling,
put on your shiny boots,
clumpy and dewy,

and meet me
by some water –
whether in full spate,

underground,
or even
dried up and lamented –

as long as
there is enough of it
to string the measure of a proper line.

Diaries and Letters

Most of these things I can no longer say,
Breeding demands I withdraw from the fray;
I went by the credo of Noblesse Oblige,
Knew all the steps and danced them with ease.
But shamed am I now for once having stated
My fear of rule by the uneducated;
Heart and mind, though willing, won't mesh,
I can't quite abide the proles in the flesh.

Moulded in Stowe and the Welsh Fusiliers
For this less than Great Britain allow me some tears.
No need to inform me we're in a new show,
I come with good manners but am now to know
Those from downstairs will attain no content
Till I'm turfed from my castle to rot in a tent.

News That Stays News

Giant Irish wind farms to power UK News Report

The flat boggy windless Irish Midlands
The flat and boggy windless Irish Midlands
The boggy, flat and windless Irish Midlands
The windless and flat and boggy Irish Midlands
The flat, boggy and windless Irish Midlands

V

Fugue from "Le Tombeau de Couperin"
(Ravel)

because the days stretched out then
because there was no hurry
because there couldn't be a hurry if I'd wanted one
because I gazed onto the wet lawn
because sometimes I gazed out there for twenty minutes
because the same pair of blackbirds came back
because I heard nothing outside
because we repeated a ten piece jigsaw twenty times
because you repeated the same first word for three weeks
because I got used to it and wasn't lonely anymore
because I couldn't get beyond just calling it beautiful
because some of these words I used in poems I wrote then
because it seems now I heard
nothing but this through your babyhood
because music is the apotheosis of poetry
and love for it cannot be written down
because *Forlane* followed like spring, *Riguadon*
a marching game, *Menuet* your afternoon sleep

Home Horizons

Walking between the trees on the root-
ruptured path, I look back and down
to the common where yesterday
we kicked and chased a football
light as a kite in the New Year's wind.
Again the clouds are low, the pitches
churned to mud and the traffic an enclosing
four sided hum. A confined unlovely space
but when your arms reached up for the lightest
brightest ball in its lurch and swirl above you
it stretched in my mind to a boundless plain.
Freedom lies at the bottom of our street
and walking between the trees I know
my nearest horizons are my furthest too.

Nativity

I took the hour off work, arrived to find
standing room only at the back of the hall.

I strained to hear, read the tiny narrator's lips:
wrapped in swaddling clothes and laid in a manger.

A cardboard wing fell off, a golden halo slipped;
one parent nudged another, giggles were suppressed.

And tears were wiped away
and then we shuffled off.

I drove the four miles back to work,
all the way tasting words:

mild, meek, mother;
hearing that voice that couldn't carry,

borne with me into the city, innocence
entreating experience to take a shepherd's part.

Blackberry picking, 11th September 2001

We'll go blackberry picking
when you come in from school

And we did. Promises to a child.
You keep the small ones.

First scorings augured a modest crop
but reaching through the tangle

we found clusters
of deepest dark

and close to their flourishings
the healthy hard potential of green.

Away and on, our movement trembled
on the briar all dappled unready fruit.

The Under 13s

For Josh

Corralled this past hour
between white lines in a field,
you peel away

from the trudge back to cars
and the overweight man
with no voice left.

Dashing to push open
the low red gate
you dive to earth

from the tops of slides,
hurl the roundabout
and orbit madly

every planet
in the fenced firmament.
You are nearly too old for this,

but for now –
cool is so uncool,
cool is *so* next year.

The Thousand-bit Jigsaw

You were musing on the clusters, abandoned
by the children for sunshine and bikes.
The call came. You packed a nightbag

and raced to her bedside. Next a blur:
a mute hostile answering machine,
the nowhere of the M1.

A fortnight later the vent of grief is a dry scorch
behind the eyes, as you watch your blond sons
touched by summer, not death,

resume their rainy day project, the thousand bits
with all four sides in place and a hundred pieces
of unfathomable shadow.

Summer's End

I dawdle at dusk on the curve
of the coast. In the easeful blue

of my mood, world is nothing
save that four-year-old child

and mild old man, hunting
the shore's most beautiful shell.

A dozen times she brings
her spilling jewels to him;

on his deliberate palm a single
offering for her.

Red Admirals

Look, four
or is it five?
celebrating
the white buddleia.

Today
may be perfect
but will show
nothing lovelier.

Sheplegh Court, 11am, 13th August 2013

Workshop Poem

Think of a place in your childhood memory.
Name something you found there.
Name two people in your life at the time and imagine them there with you.

Yes, a conker I think. That will do.
I would have been – as is still my habit –
looking down into the grass,
not up into the tree.

The sun and my right thumb, the pale
stain on the nut's surface sheen.
This is where I have a Heaney moment,
hopefully later, a Heaney line.

Behind me my elder brother
playing football with his friends.
I'd been involved but no longer.
My mother is at home preparing lunch.

I'm on my haunches, concentrating
on the conker, doing the groundwork
for the poetry workshop forty years later.

So no, I want neither my brother,
nor mother with me and the conker.
I want them exactly where they were –

helpfully positioned – just as you, workshop
leader, are helpfully positioned today,
massaging my tiny epics.

You circulate a feedback form.
I think I may have positioned
all my life – a little too artfully –

those who tried to love me.
I think I may have looked
a little too long into the grass.

Snow

Everything that couldn't wait yesterday
waits today.
Like that afternoon
ten years ago

when my son
sat in front of TV
recovering evenly
from a minor illness
and I was unable
to leave the house.

And this afternoon,
the two girls opposite
smoking under
the eaves
in their pyjamas
every half hour.

Nothing withers
in my world
on days like those
and days like these.

Himself

It is the up and out hour
in November's second week.
The weather is behaving
as if it knows itself:
I am early November. I am russet, yellow
and not yet cold.
A smoky memory is on the air.
Walking back with my newspaper
I see my neighbour's son
ten yards from his door
and a hundred from me.
I have passed his group of friends
waiting on the corner,
but he is rich in dawdling time,
and a wet firework
waits to be foot nudged
into the red leaves.
In no time
he will be laughing with those boys,
but this lost browsing minute
is the blessing of dew upon him.
My greeting intrudes
and teased from his half smile, half look up –
I barely catch it – *Hiya*

It is still possible

to live as if the computer is just
that thing on your desk at work;

to play the waltz all dreamy afternoon,
to read every word of *Daniel Deronda;*

to recall the trees of childhood,
to name them with your own children;

to look into the heart of one thing,
to stand transfixed

at the side of roads leading
everywhere else and nowhere.

1st December 2014
"Cyber Monday"

Free with Today's Paper

They came fluttering down: first the Stars
followed by Dinosaurs and a World Map;

a CD of Birdsong, posters of Wild
Flowers, Butterflies and Native Trees;

pick out a Mushroom that is safe,
identify all creatures found near Ponds.

The children of our dreams
tape it all on the walls above their beds;

the real children have stomped upstairs
to play *Grand Theft Auto*

while we leaf through the second wave:
Grecian Myth and Florentine Glory,

Poets of the Canon, the Great Composers,
another World Map for adults this time;

Philosophers, one a day to console us:
the kids will improve and talk to us again.

The Dilettante

'Too beautiful to work all day' he'd say,
then ease for an acquaintance passing by

a slow, disengaged smile,
an invitation withheld.

In the sunshine he browsed the broadsheets
where from time to time his reviews appeared,

kept in cooler weather, his quiet corner
in the city's more convivial pubs.

He wasn't much taken with attics or basements,
places where scholastic stuff got strewn around.

A minor talent ran the obituary column,
whose early work showed exquisite touch.

Eight hundred words expanding on a theme –
too beautiful, too often, to work all day.

A Plea for Clemency

(or ... what I would like to do this morning)

Draw from the automated cash dispenser
the twenty pound note that represents
my verse-writing earnings this year;

enter *The Railway Hotel* and sup
at a rate of one per forty minutes,
three pints of straw coloured ale;

find my place in the Victorian novel
I am re-reading and when concentration
falters half way down pint number two

take up the newspaper I broke my note
with on the way here and read about
the cricket I watched all day yesterday;

delve in my satchel for my own poems
for which, though they fail to find favour
elsewhere, I have a private, proud conceit;

intone on the way home my favourite phrases
in thumping bardic metronome, sleep till dusk
and wake without the headache I deserve.

Things

(after reading a poetry review)

Another poet praised for noticing things –
of the commonplace, the crystalline he sings.
I wonder one day will it be left unsaid –
the power, the power of the thing not said?

Melancholy, that privileged vapour
mingling in the huge sad cloud to pour
its precise, precise and stinging little hymns
onto a world that just gets on with things.

But things, things, there will always be things –
the spindly ragged elegance of green
sprouting from decade-cold warehouse flues;

that old cricketer behind the boundary rope.

I guess he's just my thing and why my verse
comes in minor keys, unsaid, unread.

In Memory of David Kershaw

Grammarian, Botanist, Teacher

You loved Hopkins' sonnet –
Nothing is so beautiful as spring
I wasn't so taken
with such plain declaration
though I reach now
for such a tone.

David, nothing is so beautiful
as this year's spring –
now that I have learnt
to look:

so salad green,
so sappy fresh
as the maple and lime
putting forth
outside my window.

Two years ago
we walked by the Derwent.
You named every wild flower
on the river wall.

Later, over lunch
in the pub garden
we argued about semi-colons;
Bernard's eyebrows scuttled
to the high cumulus,
but you know don't you?...
you knew, you knew...
students adored you for that.

I gaze across
May's flourishings –
all this juice and all this joy
Name for me David
the ones I still don't know.

6th May 2016

Gerard Manley Hopkins (1884-1889)   *Spring*

Further Notes on a Contributor

1. Identity Theft

Someone has stolen my identity.
I have spent far too much time off-line.

Deft thief, I wish you well
and luck with your fresh dilemmas:

Will you buy that Anita Brookner novel
I read three chapters of in the doctor's?

Shall you re-arrange the bedroom for a view
of the birch or the aspen tree?

Will you finally decide to get to grips
once and for all

with David Foster Wallace –
not just the Roger Federer bit,

or accept yourself
and read *Great Expectations* again?

Will those arguably true but needlessly cruel words
I said to her continue to nag your conscience?

When you have decided,
may I have my identity back?

You see, I need a little help
to face this world, but not too much.

2. Reading

For a decade from my mid-teens,
I filled in Application forms

with a final section entitled
'Interests' or 'Other Interests'.

I went for the classic balance:
Theatre Sport Current Affairs

and – my authentic stroke – *Reading*.
The complicating decades followed:

thinking about what I was reading,
writing about what I was reading.

I have returned to *Reading*.
Hours and hours, days and days,

weeks and weeks of reading
in a room by an A Road;

closing the window for quiet,
opening the window for air.

Afternoon, then the evening, the night:
lying in silent language,

in flowing, fleecy pillows
of paragraphs, pages,

dreaming reams and reams and reams
of reading, reading, reading.

Acknowledgements

Thanks are due to the editors of the following publications and websites in which some of these poems, or earlier versions, first appeared:

Alan Sillitoe website, Barnet Open Poetry, *Critical Survey*, Fire River Poets, *Nottingham Evening Post, Orbis, Rialto, South Bank Poetry, Staple, The Interpreter's House, The Penniless Press*, Torbay Poetry Festival website, Ver Poets, Ware Poets.

Three poems in Section II first appeared as part of *Bed Time Reading* (Five Leaves, 2011)

An earlier version of "Lest We Channel Hop" appeared in *Contains Mild Peril* (Five Leaves, 2008)

"Blackberry picking, 11th September 2001" first appeared in *One Man Queue* (Leafe Press)

Cover illustration: Bob Moulder